BUSINESS REPLY MAIL

FIRST CLASS MAIL   PERMIT NO. 1540   NASHVILLE, TN

POSTAGE WILL BE PAID BY ADDRESSEE

THE UPPER ROOM
1908 Grand Avenue
P.O. Box 189
Nashville, Tennessee 37202-9929

BUSINESS REPLY MAIL

FIRST CLASS MAIL   PERMIT NO. 1540   NASHVILLE, TN

POSTAGE WILL BE PAID BY ADDRESSEE

THE UPPER ROOM
1908 Grand Avenue
P.O. Box 189
Nashville, Tennessee 37202-9929

Weavings

"Woven together in love"

CONTENTS

editor's introduction

A S THE DAYS DARKEN and the chill of winter spreads over the land, we enter a season of waiting, a time of watching for things hidden from all eternity in the mind of God. But what unfolds before us as we await the feast of Christmas is not a charming nativity scene aglow with unearthly light. In many Western lectionaries from ancient times to the present, the Gospel texts selected for the first Sunday in Advent thunder with urgent warnings about the final coming of Jesus Christ: "There will be dreadful portents and great signs from heaven" (Luke 21:11); "Keep awake therefore, for you do not know on what day your Lord is coming" (Matt. 24:42); "Beware, keep alert" (Mark 13:33). It is as if only the strong language of the end time, the time of reckoning and rescue, the time of tearing down and creating anew, could convey the depth and breadth of meaning compressed into that tiny life lying in a feed trough. The meaning is easy enough to miss amidst all that occupies us during the holiday season. And so the Gospel texts call out: "Beware, keep alert."

How do we remain alert for the signs of God's entrance into our lives and the life of our time? What can keep us awake in the drowsy atmosphere of habit that cozily blankets our days? According to Paul, the answer is gratitude. To the Colossians he writes, "Devote yourselves to prayer, keeping alert in it with thanksgiving" (Col. 4:2). Paul is here pointing to the profound relation between spiritual alertness and the act of offering thanks. Gratitude refreshes our mind with the memory of God's gracious ways and sharpens our desire as well as our capacity to "see the goodness of the Lord in the land of the living" (Psalm 27:13). Gratitude gathers us into that double helix of grace descending and praise ascending that forms the basic design of life with God. Gratitude is the gesture of a heart opened to receive God, a heart acquainted with the shape of things to come, a heart alert to the tremors of a new creation in the birthing.

Advent begins with the end of time and ends with the beginning of God's time among us in the flesh of our common humanity. Gratitude, the wellspring of vigilance, embraces ends and beginnings. Our issue begins, therefore, with Susan Mangam's meditation on the "courteous interchange" of life and death that both sustains creation and reveals it as a "gift of love outpoured." In the infinite courtesy of love, gratitude finds its source and its most proper object. John Koenig provides the biblical framework for our issue by placing gratitude within the larger movement of praise and thanksgiving that constitute the very heartbeat within the New Testament. John shows us that the New Testament is indeed a "guidebook for eucharistic (thankful) living." Life around the family table and life in intentional community offer occasions to explore further dimensions of gratitude. Michael Williams describes the lessons his young daughter taught him about the simplicity, spontaneity, and delight that characterize genuine gratitude. Henri Nouwen recalls the departure of friends from Daybreak community and reflects on the relationship between gratitude and mission. Poems by Ruthann Johansen and Wendell Berry trace other facets of gratitude, while reviews by Rebecca Marnhout, William Moremen, and Judith Smith introduce further resources for nourishing a grateful heart.

The strange and distressing Gospel readings that inaugurate this winter season of holy waiting advise vigilance, but they also teach that nothing in life should be taken for granted. Great human achievements, like the Temple in Jerusalem, can become rubble (Luke 21:5-6); ordinary forms of human companionship can be disrupted without notice (Mt. 24:40-41); even those cosmic immutables, the sun and the stars, can come undone (Mark 13:34-35). All of life is gift, and our most fitting response to this is gratitude for what Romano Guardini calls "all the hidden and holy bonds between the Creator and ourselves."[1] Through gratitude we see with ever greater clarity that these hidden and holy bonds become flesh of our flesh and bone of our bone in the child of Bethlehem, who cinches us securely to God's own fullness of life.

John S. Mogabgab
Editor

---

[1] Romano Guardini, *Prayer in Practice* (Garden City, NY: Doubleday & Co., 1963), pp. 72–73.

contributors

WENDELL BERRY is an educator and author of numerous books of poetry and essays. He makes his home in Kentucky.

RUTHANN KNECHEL JOHANSEN is a writer who teaches at the University of Notre Dame. She has published *Coming Together: Male and Female in a Renamed Garden,* is currently completing a book on Flannery O'Connor's fiction, and is working on a new book on the role of narratives and mythology in self-reconstruction following traumatic brain injury.

JOHN KOENIG is professor of New Testament at General Theological Seminary in New York City and the author of *Rediscovering New Testament Prayer, Charismata: God's Gift for God's People, Jews and Christians in Dialogue,* and *New Testament Hospitality.*

SUSAN MANGAM, S.T.R., is an artist and a hermit residing at Christ in the Mountain Hermitage in upstate New York. She is a solitary in the Episcopal diocese of Albany, New York.

REBECCA MARNHOUT is the interim assistant editor for *Weavings.* She lives in Nashville, Tennessee, where, when she is not assisting *Weavings,* she operates a freelance editing business serving medical and religious publishers.

WILLIAM MOREMEN is a United Church of Christ minister on the staff of the Pacific Center for Spiritual Formation in northern California. He has written numerous book reviews for *Weavings.*

HENRI J. M. NOUWEN is a Roman Catholic priest of the Diocese of Utrecht, Holland. He is a spiritual director of Daybreak, the L'Arche community near Toronto, Canada. Widely known as a speaker and retreat leader, he has a special interest in Latin America and has made several trips to that region. He is the author of numerous books, most recently *The Return of the Prodigal Son*.

JUDITH E. SMITH is associate general secretary for interpretation of The United Methodist Board of Higher Education and Ministry. She is a clergy member of the Oregon-Idaho Annual Conference and is a frequent contributor to *Weavings*.

MICHAEL E. WILLIAMS is associate minister of Belle Meade United Methodist Church in Nashville, Tennessee. He holds a Ph.D. in religion/speech and theater from Northwestern University. He has involved storytelling in his ministry of preaching, teaching, liturgy, and pastoral care. He and his wife are the parents of two daughters.

DAVID KLEIN

Sing *to the* Lord *a* New Song

by Susan Mangam, S.T.R.

HARRY HAS LOST his dominance. His son has just taken over. It is hard to see the once proud little bantam huddle in the corner behind the hens. I am tempted to interfere, but past experience teaches me that these creatures will work it out for the best. They know how to be who they are. May I let them be chickens. After all, it is I, the human being, who need to learn who I am.

In many ways I only began to learn this lesson in my middle years. Memorable in this education is the day when I lay face down on the monastery floor during the chanting of the *Veni Creator.* Suddenly a powerful image of all creation rushed in through the soles of my feet, out the top of my head, on through the bishop and the altar beyond, and into the cruciform icon of Christ on the apse wall.

This vision is gradually revealing itself to be the image of God in each and every aspect of the creation. The God I once thought of only as the transcendent Wholly Other is becoming ever more present to me in the smell of the mauve earth after the frost leaves it, in the taste of the first sun-warm tomato, in the ground aglow with fallen leaves, in the silence of the creek when the ice closes it over. A wondrous paradox—the spiritual life is earthy.

COURTEOUS INTERCHANGE

AT THE HEART of my earthy existence is my participation in the cycles of mutual sacrifice that sustain all living beings. The poet Wendell Berry says, "To live we must daily break the body and shed the blood of creation." This is cause for great thanksgiving. But sadly, we humans tend to see ourselves as consumers only and not as sustainers of life, and blindly we violate this courteous interchange.

When I first moved to these mountains, I set up my wood stove and began cutting down nearby deadwood. Then I decided to clear out some young trees beginning to overtake the old orchard out back. It became a mindless routine of cutting, piling brush, stacking wood. Having just cut through one sapling, I stepped back to watch it fall. What I saw, slowly falling, was a beautiful, tall, straight black cherry whose silky skin was burgundy colored—the color of my prayer garment. And it came to me that in my trying to make the orchard conform to my ideas, I had acted carelessly and so had killed a part of myself.

We are facing a winter of great darkness and great hope on our planet: darkness, because Earth is critically wounded; hope, because we begin to be aware of our responsibility. Thomas Berry diagnoses the Earth's illness and prescribes a cure: "If the earth does grow inhospitable toward human presence, it is primarily because we have lost our sense of courtesy toward the earth and its inhabitants, our sense of gratitude, our willingness to recognize the sacred character of habitat, our capacity for the awesome, for the luminous quality of every earthly reality. We need to present ourselves to the planet as the planet presents itself to us, in an evocatory rather than a dominating relationship. There is need for great courtesy toward the earth."[1]

Healing the planet necessarily leads to self-healing, as I discovered for myself a few years ago, when I went to the Maine coast to camp in the quiet off-season. I wanted to breathe the salt air and do some drawing, but more, simply to sit on a rock at the meeting of land and sea and let the ocean give me perspective, heal me. It had always worked. But this time was different, for I felt no healing. I felt nothing. Distressed and fearing I had lost touch with the sea, my mother, I tried to draw. It came hard, as though something were wrong with me. Somehow I stuck it out, not knowing what was going on. Day after day I drew, and it seemed all darkness and chaos. Gradually, I began to come to myself and to listen. The sea was telling me I am no longer a child. I can no longer just demand, "You fix me and make me better." I was learning that the sea and I are one. This salty life-fluid of Earth is in my veins. By it I was baptized. Now I was being called to return this gift of life to the sea, my sister—to complete the cycle of courtesy. As I open myself to healing, Earth heals; as Earth heals, I heal.

---

[1]Thomas Berry, *The Dream of the Earth* (San Francisco: Sierra Club, 1988), pp. 2, 14.

TRANSFORMING POWER OF LOVE

A TREE BROUGHT ME face-to-face with my own destructiveness. Another tree, carelessly cut and fashioned into a cross, became by the transforming power of love the tree of life. By sacrificial love, every created being, from the tiniest atom to the farthest galaxy, journeys the way of the cross for the sake of new life.

The way of the cross is in each creature, faithful to its kind, participating in the cycles of mutual sacrifice. It is in the old rooster, faithful to how he is created, losing dominance to his son. It is in the rotting plant, the decaying body, returning to the soil to nurture future life. It is the path of life, death, and resurrection. The way of the cross is, day by day, to bear the burden of becoming who I really am—the person God creates. This is a process of dying to whatever blocks me from transforming love: carelessness, possessiveness, human arrogance—anything that separates me from any other being.

Thomas Merton was aware of the need to die to illusion—all that stifles the reality of God living in me—in order to become free "to enter by love into union with the Life *The* that dwells and sings within every creature and in the core of our own souls."[2] Creation is the process of *spiritual* love ever emptying into new life. In the beginning, love emptied into the void in the form of hydrogen. *life is* Hydrogen, by the transforming power of love, gave birth to helium. Through cycles of life, death, and resurrec- *earthy* tion, love poured into galaxies, our solar system, Earth, into water, air, and plant life, into reptile, bird and animal life; and love emptied into human life. All enter life by love because we are loved. In Jesus is the revelation of who we really are: love incarnate, in flesh and blood. In him the reality of every created being is revealed: "Christ is all and is in all" (Col. 3:11, NEB).

Jesus calls us to this fullness of life: "Unless a grain of wheat falls into the earth and dies, it remains alone; but if it dies it bears much fruit" (John 12:24, RSV). Unless we humans enter by love into the Earth community, we have no life. This is true not only in the outward, material aspect but also in the inward, spiritual

---

[2] William H. Shannon, *Thomas Merton's Dark Path* (New York: Farrar, Strauss, & Giroux, 1981), p. 45.

aspect of our being; for it is here, in the Earth community, that we live in Christ. Again, if we die to enslaving illusions—to all that separates us from the reality of God living in every creature—we are free to enter by love into life eternally unfolding. By the way of the cross we come into communion with all creation—the body of the risen Christ.

And as one who was dead and is alive again, we behold all as gift. The air we breathe, the trees and rocks and waters, the living and the dying, what we eat and drink, this wondrous interchange—all is the gift of love outpoured. And our hearts overflow in gratitude.

We enter as a newborn into a holy communion in which each being unfolds a unique and irreplaceable revelation of God-love. Now, in the one and only response to love, we sing, in harmony with diverse voices, creation's song of thanksgiving:

> *I will thank you because I am marvelously made;*
> *Your works are wonderful, and I know it well.*[3]

NEW LIFE

YEAR AFTER YEAR in the springtime, I watch my neighbor's cows—watching for one who begins to withdraw from the herd and get that inward look. And when she doesn't show up at the barn for feeding time, I search the pastures and woods. I suppose it is part curiosity, part concern, and still a bit of human arrogance that assumes she won't make it without me (though only once in all these years did a cow need any help in giving birth). Most times I find the cow already crooning and licking over a little, wet, glistening white-faced creature. I've learned not to get too close; mama can be quite protective. For a few hours, mama and baby are alone. The calf is scrubbed and scrubbed. It stands, falls, stands, and learns which end of mama is full of milk. Then, side by side, they begin their first journey together. Ordinarily they stop as they near the herd, and mama steps back and presents her child. One by one, cows come to greet the newborn with a gentle sniff.

On a cold, rainy morning last spring, big old "Gramma" didn't

---

[3] Psalm 139:13, *The Book of Common Prayer* (New York: The Episcopal Church, 1979), p. 795.

show up at the barn. After a long, wet search, I found her way down in the woods with her newborn. I stopped a way off. Gramma looked at me, sang that low sweet sound, stepped back, and presented him to me. Never before had this happened to me—this sacred ritual of infinite courtesy. And after I, on my knees in the mud, had joyfully caressed the new life, and Gramma and he were heading to meet the others, I thought, "I'm a cow!" No. Gramma and I know differently. But I'm no longer an intruder: I am one with them!

★   ★   ★

NOW IT IS DARK WINTER, the time of gestation, when year after year we await the coming of new life. A young woman about to give birth and her husband seek hospitality and find it, not among human society, but in a cave with cattle. After the child is born and has a time of intimacy with his mother, he is presented in the animals' feeding trough. He is greeted by lowing sounds and warm breath from gentle muzzles. And as the invisible forces of the universe commune with the visible, those humans who are in harmony with Creation—the earth, sheep, plant life; the heavens, stars, planets, cosmic life—come to this cave singing praise and thanksgiving to the God of infinite courtesy.

Morning Grace

by Ruthann Knechel Johansen

Light emerges gingerly

pushing the mottled night comforter

aside.

Bending the stillness,

calling forth winds,

light fully awake

tosses trees behind my head

into alluring dances on the wall I face.

And I barefoot return

grateful salutations.

The Heartbeat *of* Praise *and* Thanksgiving

by John Koenig

A TALLY OF PASSAGES in the New Testament that describe or encourage the praising of God and Christ yields a number well over two hundred. When we consider that the New Testament is rather a small book and contains no liturgical manual like the Old Testament Psalter, this number looms quite large. Furthermore, the words used for acts of praise turn out to be extraordinary in their variety. In addition to the verb "praise" itself, the following expressions occur: bless, thank, worship, glorify, fall on one's face, kneel, honor, magnify, extol, rejoice in, confess, acknowledge, sing hymns and psalms to, offer gifts or sacrifices, boast in, speak in tongues, invoke, present or yield oneself to, be devoted to, live to, declare the mighty works of, and sanctify the Name. Special words of acclamation like Hosannah, Hallelujah, and Amen are found throughout the New Testament, while the Revelation of John in particular abounds with outbursts of praise like "Holy, Holy, Holy," "Worthy art thou," and "We give thanks to thee, Lord God Almighty." Moreover, scholars have identified hymnlike poems and doxologies in the Gospels and several of the epistles (Lk. 1:46-55, 68-79; 2:29-32; Jn. 1:1-18; Rom. 11:33-36; Phil. 2:5-11; Col. 1:15-20; 1 Tim. 3:16). The consensus is that these are not simply literary pieces but were actually used in the worship of the earliest church.

How shall we account for this great outpouring of praise language? Perhaps the best answer is to recall that the New Testament grew out of something it calls the gospel, the good news of what God did and does through Jesus. The first believers seem to have spent a great deal of time thanking God for the renewal of their lives in Christ and passing this joy on to others in the form of gospel proclamation (see Acts 2:1-47, which begins and ends with praise) or reflection (Rom. 1:8-17). In fact, the New Testament functions as a kind of guidebook for eucharistic (thankful) living. It reflects the conviction of the earliest believers that whatever their communities said and did was to be offered up in gratitude for the saving guidance of the Holy Spirit, an experience they traced directly to God's raising of Jesus from the dead (Acts 2:32-33). In this vein, the author of Ephesians urges his readers to "be filled with the Spirit, addressing one another with psalms and hymns and spiritual songs, singing and making melody to the Lord with all your heart, always and for everything [or on behalf of all people] giving thanks in the name of our Lord Jesus Christ to God the Father" (5:18-20). If we can talk of something like a heartbeat within the New Testament, a pulsating center that pumps life to the whole body, it is properly named by the words *praise* and *thanksgiving*.

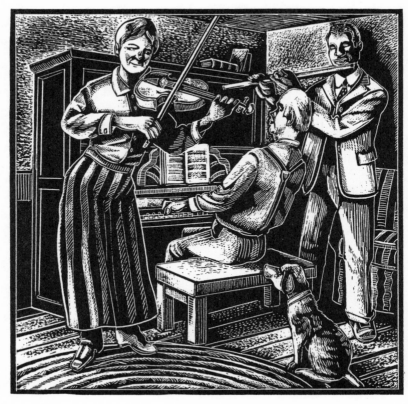

Praise is the comprehensive term for all the words and music and bodily motions we use in ascribing ultimate worth to God, simply because of who God is. Thanksgiving is a type of praise. It means spelling out the details of God's redemptive work in our lives and expressing our gratitude for them. The New Testament contains many references to the blessing of God by humans, but it is the language of thanksgiving that predominates in our canonical Gospels and epistles. One reason for this distinctive feature of New Testament praising emerges from the very structure of the word *eucharistia*. It is constructed from the Greek *charis*, meaning "grace," and the prefix *eu*, which means "good" or "well." Thus we might think of *eucharistia* and the verb *eucharisteo* as a "speaking well of grace." Because the New Testament believers felt God's grace so intensely in the forgiveness, healing, and strength of purpose that God had granted them, they delighted in it among themselves and offered up their words and songs about it as *eucharistia*. It is no exaggeration to claim that this wondrous spiral of grace descending and thanks ascending forms the very axis of Christian faith.

PRAY CONSTANTLY, WITH THANKSGIVING

THAT IS WHY several New Testament writers can exhort us to do something that seems quite impossible for ordinary people immersed in busy lives, that is, pray constantly. If grace truly abounds, then thanksgiving, in the New Testament view of things, becomes a natural inclination toward offering ourselves to God. Thanksgiving is more than a pleasant feeling, spontaneously and effortlessly expressed in word or song. Clearly we should not exclude this kind of exuberance (and most of us have a great deal to learn about it from the black and pentecostal churches). But since thanksgiving is commanded, it must reside more in the realm of obedience and discipline than in the emotions as such. We might say that thanksgiving lives just beneath the ordinary awareness of believers but is always ready with the Spirit's urging and our cooperation, to rush forth into sound. For maturing Christians, praise and thanksgiving are a kind of foundation for their everyday perception and decision making.

Paul says that we are to rejoice in the Lord always and give thanks in every situation. Furthermore, whatever we *do* is to be accompanied by thanksgiving. If this counsel is anything more than pure exaggeration, an element of choice is involved. We must *decide* to offer up our gratitude. Yet our conscious resolution alone, distracted by the many thoughts and events of the day, will not suffice to accomplish this. Precisely in giving thanks we do not know how to pray as we ought but must rely on the Spirit's aid (Rom. 8:26). Still, the constant offering of gratitude is a goal toward which our life of prayer can move, even as we quite properly focus on our daily responsibilities.

Praise is the doorway to blessed assurance

In recent years I have become acquainted with a busy young woman, an attorney and general counsel for a large corporation. And I have learned to respect her faith. Once I asked her if she could describe her prayer life for me. She seemed bemused by the question and at first answered that she didn't pray all that much. But then she corrected herself and said, "Well, maybe I do pray rather often, though not always in words. I guess I would call it adoration." This second-thought response makes a great deal of sense to me.

How can we walk more confidently in the path of thanksgiving? In her article "Marathons, Daily Races, and Thanksgiving," Margaret Wold maintains that it is "not the big crises that devastate our faith in the reality of God. It's the wearisome progression of days and nights full of cares and pressures."[1] As an antidote to this constant chipping away at our trust, Wold recommends the repeated use of many short prayers. Most other examples have to do with petitionary prayer, but toward the end of her essay she moves toward what we have called the heartbeat of praise and thanksgiving. I think we can all seek and find many occasions during the course of an average day when we can honestly say, "Thanks be to God" or "Praise the Lord" or whatever seems right to us to verbalize our gratitude. This practice may seem awkward at first, but if we continue with it the number of occasions is likely to grow.

To be sure, concerns for "undivided devotion to the Lord" (1 Cor. 7:35) can degenerate into an obsessive-compulsive behavior in which words of praise become magic charms, necessary to maintain our mental balance. For most of us, however, this is not a real danger; and if it becomes so, a spiritual director or good friend can help us to let go of it. From a New Testament point of

---

[1] *The Lutheran*, November 23, 1988, 19.

view, the more serious pathology consists in not giving thanks at all, or only rarely.

"Give thanks in every situation" (1 Thess. 5:18). This discipline is harder, for even when we feel anxious or depressed or angry we need to trust that the Spirit is working within us to help us acknowledge God's redeeming presence. Even in our afflictions we must listen for the still, small voice that tells us, "Right now is a good time to give thanks, for the grace of Jesus Christ is restoring you, and it will accomplish far more than you ask or think."

Some writers on prayer hold that praise and thanksgiving ought to be offered not only *in* every situation but *for* every situation.[2] As far as I can tell, the only New Testament support for this view occurs in Eph. 5:20, where readers are urged to give thanks "always and for everything." But this phrase could also be translated "on behalf of everyone," so it may refer to an intercessory type of thanksgiving like the one Paul offers in Phil. 1:3-11. Even if we adopt the standard translation, we should probably understand it in the light of 1 Thess. 5:18, so that it comes to mean something like "We give thanks to you, O God, even for this terrible time, but only because we trust that you are in it, working for the good of us all and sanctifying to us our deepest distress." God asks for the sacrifice of praise and thanksgiving, but not for the sacrifice of our honesty.

FOR GOD'S SAKE, AND THE KINGDOM

JESUS TELLS A SAMARITAN WOMAN, "The hour is coming, and now is, when the true worshipers will worship the Father in spirit and truth, for such the Father seeks to worship him"(Jn. 4:23). We do not put it too strongly when we say that God longs for our full attention, embodied in words and songs of praise. We praise because God desires us to praise, and so we come to share in the very joy of heaven. The young Scottish university student in the film *Chariots of Fire* must have felt this when he said of God: "It pleasures Him that I run like the wind."

But the praise of God involves something more than our good feelings. In maturing believers it always progresses to adora-

---

[2] Probably the best-known representative of this position is Merlin R. Carothers. See especially *Power in Praise: How the Spiritual Dynamic of Praise Revolutionizes Our Lives* (Plainfield, NJ: Logos International, 1971).

tion. "Gratitude exclaims, very properly, 'How good of God to give me this.' Adoration says, 'What must be the quality of that Being whose far-off and momentary coruscations are like this!' One's mind runs back up the sunbeam to the sun."[3] God wants this reflective admiration, and those who love God will be constrained by love to offer it, to "sing psalms and hymns and spiritual songs with thankfulness in [their] hearts to God" (Col. 3:16). This rule applies even to times of trial. Thus we learn from Acts 16:25 that the imprisoned Paul and Silas, still bleeding from cruel blows at the hands of Roman officials, sing praises to God with midnight hymns. But whatever our circumstances, we can be sure that we are never alone in our praying. Jesus intercedes for us and even leads our praises (Rom. 15:7-11; Heb. 2:12). He stirs up the Holy Spirit within us to fashion our words and melodies. Here too we pray through him, or in his name (Col. 3:17; Eph. 5:20; 1 Thess. 5:18).

Often we find passages in the Old and New Testaments that may be called doxologies, that is, ascriptions of glory to God from humans. One of the chief songs in our eucharistic liturgy has been named the Gloria. It derives from a number of biblical texts but especially from Luke's account of the angels' song at Jesus' birth ("Glory to God in the highest," Lk. 2:14). A similar picture comes from Paul's letter to the Philippians, where the apostle quotes from an early Christian hymn that ends with these words: "Therefore God has highly exalted him [Jesus] and bestowed on him the name which is above every name, that at the name of Jesus every knee should bow, in heaven and on earth and under the earth, and every tongue confess that Jesus Christ is Lord, to the glory of God the Father" (2:9-11). Paul and his readers were quite aware that this cosmic acknowledgment had not yet happened. But they offered up their hymn to anticipate the fullness of that which was already dawning.

In fact some New Testament believers appear to hold the view that they can hasten the divine triumph by magnifying God's glory in their praise, especially when they render it in the name of Jesus. Thus Paul writes that we are to "utter the Amen through [Christ], to the glory of God" (2 Cor. 1:20), and this probably refers to a real liturgical practice. When Christians say "Amen!" they visualize the life and work of Jesus and offer them up to God in a way that somehow enhances the divine stature. Paul understands his whole

---

[3] C. S. Lewis, *Letters to Malcolm*, 90.

ministry to be moving toward one goal: "that as grace extends to more and more people it may increase thanksgiving [for our share in Christ's resurrection] to the glory of God" (2 Cor. 4:15; see also 1:11 and 9:11-15). For the New Testament writers, praise is no side issue. Those graced by the Holy Spirit to confess Jesus as Lord must be especially zealous in speaking and singing their thanks to God *for the very sake of God's Personhood.*

But this Personhood can never be separated from the destiny of creation. God's consummate will is to share divine glory with everything that exists. In the interim time before Christ's return to judge the nations, God grants visions of this final glory, allows us to touch and sense it in our hearts (2 Cor. 3:18; 4:6; 4:17-5:5). But at the same time we are enjoined to return it, with thanksgiving, so that the plan of God can move forward (2 Cor. 4:15). We have learned that when we pray, "Thy kingdom come," our petition has an actual effect on God's working out of the world's salvation. In the same way our praise and thanksgiving contribute tangibly to the healing of the cosmos.

Prayer with thanksgiving gives us access to a profound well-being

Daniel Hardy and David Ford conclude that "praise . . . is best seen as part of an ecology of blessing." What they mean is that while the whole world renders homage to God in and of itself, we humans are uniquely gifted as the poets and priests of creation. We are called to articulate the worship it offers, along with our own, in fresh new ways, thus becoming what George Herbert called "secretaries of [God's] praise."[4] The Judeo-Christian tradition as a whole teaches that every human being is a special herald of God's presence in his or her own corner of the universe. Some stand out as exemplars of praise, schoolmasters of worship for the rest of humanity. Johann Sebastian Bach was one of these. His biographers tell us that he always inscribed the words "Soli Deo Gloria" (to God alone be the glory) on his working manuscripts, even on the scores we now call secular. Those who know Bach's life and music well agree that for him these words were no pious convention but a real prayer that the notes he inked would rise as a melody to the Lord.[5]

---

[4]Daniel W. Hardy and David F. Ford, *Praising and Knowing God* (Philadelphia: Westminster Press, 1985), 82. The phrase comes from Herbert's poem "Providence."

[5]Jaroslav Pelikan, *Bach Among the Theologians* (Philadelphia: Fortress Press, 1986), 140.

In the New Testament praise of God on behalf of the world is always mediated through Jesus, who is confessed as "the image of the invisible God" (Col. 1:15-20). In this hymn the early church sang forth its praise, not only for the wonders of creation (which it had come to understand christologically) but also for the costly reconciliation of all things to God won by Jesus' death. These two are now inseparable. By honoring the creative-redemptive work of Christ with their voices, believers are drawn into it more deeply. It is hardly accidental that when the Risen One pours out "the promise of the Father" on his disciples at Pentecost, their very first Spirit-filled act is to proclaim God's works in ecstatic tongues of praise (Acts 2:1-11). And this praise is met with a receptiveness on the part of many onlookers that prompts the church's first missionary effort (2:12-42).

FOR OUR OWN SAKE

WE HAVE REFERRED to praise and thanksgiving as a heartbeat because they throb at the very center of our Christian faith. But we have also said that praise and thanksgiving are a discipline. A decision is required before words and songs can burst forth. Sometimes this is a natural decision, made without effort because of our overflowing gratitude for a special work of God in our lives. At other times we must struggle to praise God because we feel dry or deprived. Yet even then, when we are able to overcome our resistance, we can begin to taste joy. More than any other form of devotion, praise and thanksgiving engage our whole physical being. Music, poetry, dance, and just plain loud noise are the basic stuff of praise.

The New Testament has a good deal to tell us about the felt benefits of praise and thanksgiving. Together they may be thought of as a training course in righteousness. Through praise we learn virtue, and we discover, in ever-richer patterns, God's regenerating love for us. Thus the author of Acts tells us that when Paul, en route to Rome as a prisoner, encountered some bold Christian friends who had journeyed out from the capital to welcome him, "he thanked God and took courage" (28:16). The very sight of these believers was probably enough to lift Paul's spirits, but by voicing his gratitude to God he also found new bravery. Earlier in writing to the Romans, he himself had cited the example of Abraham, "who grew strong in his faith as he gave glory to God" (4:20). And some verses later the apostle urged his readers to present their bodies to God as a living sacrifice, to "be transformed by the renewal of your mind, that you may prove [i.e., test out in experience] what is the will of God, what is good and acceptable and perfect" (12:1-2). According to the logic of this text, thankful self-offering results in a heightened ability to discern and embrace God's purposes.

Other acts of worship are equally productive. Paul writes to the Corinthians, "The cup of blessing which we bless, is it not a participation [*koinonia*] in the blood of Christ?" (1 Cor. 10:16). Here the reference is to Holy Communion, and the major point is made in the little clause "which we bless." Obviously the saving force of Christ's blood is not dependent on human words. But Paul is telling his readers that when they speak actual blessings over the cup at the Supper of the Lord, they are joined together with Christ's offering at a new level. More than ever, they belong exclusively to the Lord (see 10:18-22).

Praise is also the trainer of our affections. When Paul urges the Philippians to "have no anxiety about anything, but in everything by prayer and supplication with thanksgiving let your requests be made known to God" (4:6), he is not making an impossible demand, on the order of "Stop being bothered." Rather, he exhorts his readers from a personal knowledge of what thanksgiving produces: "And the peace of God, which passes understanding, will keep your hearts and minds in Christ Jesus" (4:7). Prayer with thanksgiving gives us access to a profound well-being so that we no longer have to suffer domination by our troubled psyches. How different this is from the shallow comfort served up in our mass media: "Don't worry, be happy." From a quite practical point of view, the only medicine for inner turmoil is true worship. Worship offers release from the oppressive power of negative emotions. The ability to "have no fear," to "be prepared," and to make our faith statements "with gentleness and reverence" stems from a constant devotion to Christ in our heart (1 Pet. 3:14-16).

It is easy to criticize the impression given by Merlin Carothers that praising God relieves practically every affliction known to humanity. Yet the New Testament passages we have just cited show that there is something authentic in his position. Carothers rightly states that "praising God is something more than a change in our... attitude. There is no power in our words of praise as such. There is no power in our attitude.... All the power in the situation comes from God."[6] Precisely this is what we need to rediscover. Not our words or the quality of our inner devotion, but God, acting through our praise, accomplishes far more than we can ask or imagine.

Praise is paradoxical. We learn it, but we also learn from it, especially during corporate worship. In Eph. 5:19 we are urged to address one another in psalms and hymns and spiritual songs. Our melodies are directed chiefly to God (v. 19b), but at the same time they teach and build up our brother and sister worshipers. Joining in the "Amen" means that we affirm what the giver of thanks has just said or sung. We connect with it and are ourselves lifted up to God. The black churches in America know this truth. The frequent outbursts from worshipers of "Praise the Lord" or "Amen" or "Thank you, Jesus" are personal (and quite biblical) ways of appropriating the grace of God that has been manifested in sermons and prayers.

We have already mentioned the enhanced discernment of

MICHAEL McCURDY

God's will that derives from our self-offerings to our Abba (Rom. 12:1-2). It is important to highlight another benefit of such praise, namely, a deeper plunge into the vast oceans of God's mercy. Before Paul asks his readers to present their bodies as living sacrifices, he takes them through a complex meditation on God's mysterious dealings with the church and Israel (Rom. 9:1-11:32). Then, at the end of this, he leads them—for we must assume that the apostle's letter was read out loud during a period of corporate worship—in a magnificent doxology: "O the depth of the riches and wisdom and knowledge of God! How unsearchable are his judgments and how inscrutable his ways! For who has known the mind of the Lord, or who has been his counselor?... For from him and through him and to him are all things. To him be glory for ever. Amen" (11:33-36).

What happens in this section of Romans is an exponential progression of praise. We begin to see something of God's mercy and stand in awe of it (11:25-32). We offer up a doxology in thanksgiving (11:33-36). Then we are drawn by these words into a more complete self-offering (12:1-2) during which our minds are directed toward finding our own personal place in God's gracious work (12:3-8). And this results in new behavior, formed by praise: "Let love be genuine;... outdo one another in showing honor.... Be aglow with the Spirit.... Rejoice in your hope.... Bless those who persecute you.... Overcome evil with good" (12:9-21). The entire process becomes an interplay between the wideness of God's mercy and our response to it. Hardy and Ford put it beautifully when they write: "[Praise] is the life of faith, basic Christian existence, and it springs from our recognition, respect, and honoring being focused through Jesus Christ and being allowed to transform our network of relationships. Our whole life is continually thrown into the air in praise in the trust that it will be caught, blessed and returned renewed."[7] To live out that metaphor of throwing our lives into the air, even for a day, would be to experience richness beyond measure.

By choosing to entitle their book *Praising and Knowing God*, Hardy and Ford have caught hold of something absolutely essential to the Judeo-Christian understanding of praise. What we come to discover, finally, through our glorification of God in word and song, is the astonishing force of God's intimacy. It was the habit of praise that inspired the psalmist to exclaim: "Oh

[6] *Power in Praise*, 8.
[7] *Praising and Knowing God*, 76.

Lord, thou has searched me and known me (Ps. 139:1-6). We might well recoil in terror from this discovery, for it means that God intrudes upon our every thought and feeling, indeed, anticipates them before they occur. But what if this God is also our Abba who searches us in love for the sake of our healing and the growth of our freedom? It was just such a revelation, given through Christ and the Spirit, that enabled Paul to conclude: "if one loves God, then it follows that this person is known by God. . . . For we see at present through a looking glass, indirectly, but then [at the end of time] we shall see face to face. Now I know in part; but then I shall know, even as I am fully known" (1 Cor. 8:3; 13:12, my translation). It goes without saying that we can apprehend the searching love of God only imperfectly. But we can grasp enough of it to praise and thank God. And in these acts of glorification we get some real sense of knowing as we are known. Praise is the doorway to blessed assurance.

THERE IS ONE MORE FACET of New Testament praise and thanksgiving that we dare not ignore, though it may seem extremely odd and even shocking to some readers. I have in mind the early church's practice of joining its voice with the hosts of heaven to laud and honor God. We catch a glimpse of this in an extraordinary passage from Hebrews. Addressing his readers as a congregation and referring (I believe) to their regular corporate worship, the author states: "You have come to Mount Zion and to the city of the living God, the heavenly Jerusalem, and to innumerable angels in festal gathering, and to the assembly of the firstborn who are enrolled in heaven, and to a judge who is God of all, and to the spirits of just people made perfect, and to Jesus the mediator of a new covenant" (12:22-24). Does this passage really describe the church's praise now? Almost certainly it does. The Greek word translated "you have come" occurs earlier in Hebrews in a section on petitionary prayer. Having reminded his readers that they are aided by none other than Jesus himself in his role as great high priest, the author concludes: "Let us then with confidence draw near to the throne of grace, that we may receive mercy and find grace to help in time of need" (4:16). Thus prayer means approaching a special "place" within God's presence. Mount Zion stands for that part of the heavenly sanctuary where music and praise are offered to God, hence the "innumerable angels in festal gathering."

For centuries the Greek and Russian Orthodox churches,

along with several other branches of Eastern Christianity, have simply assumed, on the basis of these passages and a rich fund of worship experience, that they are offering up their praise and thanksgiving together with the heavenly hosts. Indeed, they usually refer to their order of worship as Divine Liturgy. A remnant of this tradition appears in some Western services of the Lord's Supper when the celebrant proclaims, "Therefore we praise you, joining our voices with Angels and Archangels and with all the company of heaven, who forever sing this hymn to proclaim the glory of your Name." To which the people respond: "Holy, holy, holy Lord, God of power and might, heaven and earth are full of your glory. Hosanna in the highest."[8]

What if it is all true? What if our praising matters so much to God that it draws us up into the worship of the heavenly court? If this *is* the case, some of us will have to rethink our position on angels, or on heaven itself for that matter. And here again we may also recall Jesus' imaging of God's kingdom as a festal procession that can be joined as we pray the Lord's Prayer. Praise and thanksgiving would be yet another entry into that movable feast where heaven and earth are found to intersect.

It may be that petition and intercession will always come easier to us than praise and thanksgiving. But the New Testament does not allow us to rest content with this state of affairs. If anything, the opposite is true. The profusion of praise language in our apostolic writings stands as a constant reminder that words and hymns to the glory of God must occupy a certain primacy in our life of prayer. Without them something quintessential is lost from our faith. With them the gospel begins to be embodied. Praise and thanksgiving in Jesus' name require an extra measure of boldness on our part in this era of great confusion about Christian worship. But the command is clear, the promise is sure, and the blessings are many.

---

[8] *The Book of Common Prayer* (1979). See "The Holy Eucharist, Rite II."

25

GRACE
AND
GRATITUDE
BELONG
TOGETHER
LIKE
HEAVEN
AND
EARTH.

GRACE   GRATITUDE
EVOKES   FOLLOWS
GRATITUDE   GRACE
LIKE   LIKE
THE VOICE   THUNDER
AN ECHO.   LIGHTNING.

KARL BARTH

Saying Grace:
LIVING A LIFE OF GRATITUDE

by Michael E. Williams

I BEGIN WITH A CONFESSION: I have offered thanks over meals only sporadically during my life, though I grew up in a family where saying the blessing was a ritual obligation at virtually every family meal. The practice went by several other names, offering thanks, blessing the food, and saying grace among them. Early on I embraced the blessing wholeheartedly; only later did I become haphazard in my practice of saying it.

Actually, as a small child I anointed myself protector of orthodoxy for this familial observance. A certain posture accompanied our blessing: hands folded, heads bowed, and eyes closed.

I took it upon myself to scan the faces around the table, making sure that each person followed the rules to the letter. If I saw an opened eye, I would take the offender to task for this breach of pious etiquette. I continued my little inquisition until one day I made the mistake of accusing a neighbor, Kinslo Butler, who observed in response that if I had seen his eyes open then mine must have been open too. My cheeks burned as I realized that I had been caught in my own trap, guilty of the same crime of which I was accusing another. Little did I know at the time that I was sharing the fate of those who rush to judgment. Nowadays, when my mother asks if I want to say the blessing—which is not really a request but an expectation traveling in the disguise of an invitation—I know enough to keep my eyes closed.

Later, as a teenager, a friend and I liked to create a bit of religious vaudeville around the blessing. Seated at the table of his family or mine, one of us would whisper and mumble through the offering of thanks. After the amen, the other would say in an irritated voice, "I couldn't hear you." To this the one who prayed would retort, "I wasn't talking to you." This weak attempt at humor exhausted my adolescent theological reflection on the subject of blessings at meals.

Since that time I have participated in a wide range of blessings, from "God is great, God is good," to the Hebrew blessing over the bread. I have sung thanks in the words of the doxology and the Johnny Appleseed grace. I have held hands with those around the table and have looked with neither judgment nor guilt into the eyes of others with whom I was about to share a meal. In all of these experiences I never lost the troubling sense that I was simply meeting an obligation, doing what was expected, being a good boy.

I think this is the root of my resistance to saying a blessing at meals. No matter how creative the form or lilting the language, I am still simply doing what I am supposed to do. It is an activity imposed upon me, possibly even by my own uneasy conscience. I am the sort of person who can be persuaded to go along with many things in life, but try to coerce me to do something (even something that under other circumstances I would choose to do), and I will clench my fists, grit my teeth, and refuse. My mother's word for this attitude is "contrary."

Recently my lackadaisical attitude toward the blessing has been transformed. This transformation was brought about through the good offices of neither my parents nor my favorite religious writers and teachers. Rather, my two-year-old daughter, Sarah, renewed for me the practice of saying the blessing.

One evening at dinner she thrust her hands toward her mother and me, accompanying this motion with a vigorous bow of her head. When we finally figured out that she was wanting us to take her hands and join hands ourselves, we did so and bowed our heads. When she perceived that all was ready, Sarah said, "Thank you food." Whereupon she threw her parents a look of ecstatic delight. Then in the manner of a teacher attempting to coach a particularly slow group of students, she said in tones that invited other voices to join in, "A-men."

Margaret and I discussed where our daughter had learned this blessing and decided that it must be the practice of her Parents' Day Out class at our church. But we were not prepared for the enthusiasm with which she practiced her newfound spiritual discipline. Throughout the meal she would periodically stop eating, drop her fork or spoon, and with the same thrusting of her arms prepare to offer thanks for some blessing that had just come to mind. Each time Margaret and I (like any true followers of a religious leader) would join hands, and when the circle was complete Sarah would begin again, "Thank you Mommy. Thank you Daddy. Thank you Spankie" (our cat). Each blessing would close with the same rapturous smile as she made eye contact so we could all say in unison, "A-men."

What father's heart would not be captivated by his two-year-old daughter's spontaneous offering of thanks to God for him, her mother, and even the cat? As the weeks passed the list grew to include grandparents, neighbors, and friends. While the names changed, the delight in Sarah's face never diminished.

SIMPLICITY, SPONTANEITY, DELIGHT

BEYOND THE ENCHANTMENT of these moments, I began to realize that what I was witnessing was gratitude in as pure a form as humans ever practice it. First, it was *simple*. Three words sufficed to express my daughter's thanks. She simply said, "Thank you," then named that for which she was grateful. Second, each phrase rose to the surface *spontaneously,* without prompting or any sense of obligation. Finally, Sarah's facial expression spoke more clearly than her words of the *unrestrained delight* she took in offering thanks. This is saying grace, indeed.

Simplicity is not denial of the complications of modern life.

These are irrelevant to the quality of simplicity we carry within. Simplicity is not so much an outward form of speech or manner as it is the driving heartbeat that sets the rhythm of a human life. Thomas Kelly defines simplicity as living from "a divine Center."[1] Often complications become distractions from the divine presence available to us as the center of our lives. The simplicity that characterizes this divine center allows us to make choices among the many demands on our lives.

Elaine Prevallet describes simplicity as "having a clear focus on the one thing necessary, an undivided heart."[2] The opposite of simplicity, the divided heart, seeks security in the many unnecessary things that draw attention away from the divine presence that is "the one thing necessary." Prevallet restates Jesus' warning against attempting to serve two masters when she suggests, in a play on words, that simplicity is opposite to duplicity.

True gratitude is born of simplicity

Duplicity, which denotes deception as well as doubleness, is a very necessary evil in the world of the divided heart. There, one may serve many more than two masters, all of which demand time and loyalty. These are subtle figures, often appearing as parents, teachers, bosses, even religious and spiritual leaders. We labor under the delusion that we must appease these masters so that they will reward us, or at least do us no harm. Duplicitous gratitude, or flattery, is tribute we pay to these figures of power.

If duplicity inevitably leads along the byways of dishonesty, its opposite, simplicity, leads us along the more excellent path. True gratitude is born of simplicity, since it emerges out of the single-heartedness that acknowledges one Center. When simplicity rules our heart, we offer thanks for many gifts and occasions of our lives to this single source, the divine presence in our lives. Since God will not be flattered, there is no need for flowery extravagances. A simple "Thank you" is enough.

Spontaneity is the second theme in this song of grace. The same singleness of heart that allows the melody of simplicity to emerge is also the source of the improvisation on that melodic theme that we call spontaneity. Like all improvisation, there is an unpremeditated quality about the spontaneous expression of grat-

[1] *A Testament of Devotion* (New York: Harper and Brothers, 1941), p. 116.

[2] *Reflections on Simplicity*, Pendle Hill Pamphlet 244 (Wallingford, PA: Pendle Hill Publications, 1982), p. 9.

itude. Grace is said in the moment as a response to the present situation, acknowledging the role of the divine presence that is the Center around which our lives are constellated.

The clearest description in the Bible of such an unpremeditated response is found in Jesus' parable of the final judgment in Matthew 25. After the judge of all the earth has divided the sheep from the goats, each group engages in a bit of self-revealing dialogue with the judge. When the judge lauds the sheep who offered food for his hunger, clothes for his nakedness, water for his thirst, and companionship in his times of illness and imprisonment, their response reveals the unselfconscious character of their actions: "When did we do these things for you?" Those on the judge's right responded to others' needs in a simple, spontaneous manner. They did not wonder whom their actions would please or displease. More important, they did not view their actions as obligations, and they expected no reward for performing them. They had simply responded out of the bounty they had been given. Such giving, offered in unpremeditated, spontaneous fashion, is gratitude embodied, pure and simple.

Jesus graced the dreadful evening of his betrayal with gratitude

The goats on the judge's left hand have lived their lives from a very different center. When they are chastised for not offering the judge food, water, clothing, and companionship, they reply, "If we had only known it was you, we would have responded." This is duplicity's answer to need: If only I had known that it was someone I owed gratitude to, someone who in the future could reward or punish me, then I would have responded. This suggests that every choice should be premeditated because we have to figure out whom among the many powerful figures in our life we must appease or flatter.

Unrestrained delight is a rare experience in most lives, since so many circumstances can stand in the way of our happiness. Of course, happiness is hardly a reasonable goal when it is defined as having only good things and no bad things happen to us. Bad things, from minor irritations to genuine tragedies, come to us all. Gratitude does not offer thanks only for the good things that happen. It says grace over all the occasions of our lives.

Unrestrained delight comes from a life of following the inklings that point us toward God's deepest yearnings for our lives. Such delight does not depend on the circumstances of our lives, since we recognize that every blessing is a mixed one.

Delight is not restrained by circumstances after we realize that gratitude is offering thanks for all of life's occasions, since we do not know which will turn out to be the greatest blessings.

To say grace is to respond to God's gracious gifts simply and spontaneously and with unrestrained delight. To live out these responses as well as to speak them is the very embodiment of gratitude. To say grace with our voices and our lives is to join hands with others in a community that expresses in its life together simplicity, spontaneity, and delight in one another and the creation.

TOGETHER IN JOYFUL CELEBRATION

BEFORE I WAX too rhapsodic, I must honestly say that as time has passed I am more and more convinced that in saying grace, Sarah's delight is colored by being the center of attention for the moment. At the same time I am quite sure she is truly thankful for that attention. That is why I said earlier that her "saying grace" was as pure an expression of gratitude as a human being could practice. Even our most honest attempts to be transparent to God's grace carry with them the taint of self-consciousness and self-interest. Children are just a bit more open and honest than adults are about expressing the role self plays in everything they do.

The very word "gratitude" (and its close relatives) acknowledges this tension. Both "grace" and "gratitude" have their source in the Latin word *gratia*, which can mean both favor and pleasure. Thus gratitude is not simply receiving or returning a favor (with the hint of obligation), it is also taking pleasure in some gift or relationship. From this same source, however, comes "gratuity," for a practice that seems to have begun as a free offering in gratitude for services rendered but has now become an expectation.

It is important to recognize that "gratitude" and "grace" may even go back to the ancient Sanskrit word *gurtas*, meaning religious celebration. In essence this is still what saying grace is all about, the celebration of the people, places, and things of our lives by ourselves living a life of gratitude.

For Christians the primary place where we should see such gracious living modeled is in the celebration of the Eucharist. In fact, the word "Eucharist" bespeaks a joyful celebration, rather than the severe and penitential experience many of us have at communion. At this holy meal we remember that Jesus offered thanks over the bread and wine before passing it among his disciples, of whom one had betrayed him, one would deny him, and all would desert him. Still he offered thanks, saying grace by offering up both words and his very life. Jesus graced the dreadful evening of his betrayal with gratitude.

As we gather at the table we not only remember that last supper and participate as disciples who have betrayed, denied, and deserted the one who offered his life for us. We also look forward to that banquet in a time beyond time at which all those God has loved beyond our failures will gather in joyful celebration.

Now when I join hands with Margaret and Sarah around our table at home, I feel at the same time the touch of those who have said grace in their lives and words: David dancing before the ark, Mary Magdalene recognizing her beloved in the garden, and Jesus offering thanks over a cup of blessing, even as he wished with all his soul that the bitter draught of crucifixion might pass him by.

Recently a new set of hands was added to our circle. Several weeks ago Sarah's sister, Elizabeth, was born. Margaret and I were not at all sure that her birth would be an occasion about which Sarah would be grateful. After all, until Elizabeth came along Sarah had been the sole focus of all our love and attention. We were pleasantly surprised when Sarah seemed to genuinely care for her baby sister, though her behavior toward us varied from being much more clinging to being downright standoffish.

During a recent dinner Sarah began her meal-long procedure of saying grace after making less of a fuss than we had expected over her parents' difficulty completing the circle of hands because one of us was holding Elizabeth. A short time later, in the midst of the meal, she startled us further when she added a variation on the blessing we had not heard before: "Thank you Libess." And the people of God gathered around that table shared the almost unutterable delight written on this older sister's face, as we all said, "A-men!"

The Gift of Gravity

by Wendell Berry

All that passes descends,
and ascends again unseen
into the light: the river
coming down from sky
to hills, from hills to sea,
and carving as it moves,
to rise invisible,
gathered to light, to return
again. "The river's injury
is its shape." I've learned no more.
We are what we are given
and what is taken away;
blessed by the name
of the giver and taker.
For everything that comes
is a gift, the meaning always
carried out of sight
to renew our whereabouts,
always a starting place.
And every gift is perfect
in its beginning, for it

is "from above, and cometh down
from the Father of lights."
Gravity is grace.
All that has come to us
has come as the river comes,
given in passing away.
And if our wickedness
destroys the watershed,
dissolves the beautiful field,
then I must grieve and learn
that I possess by loss
the earth I live upon
and stand in and am. The dark
and then the light will have it.
I am newborn of pain
to love the new-shaped shore
where young cottonwoods
take hold and thrive in the wound,
kingfishers already nesting
in a hole in the sheared bank.
"What is left is what is"—
have learned no more. The shore
turns green under the songs
of the fires of the world's end,
and what is there to do?
Imagine what exists
so that it may shine
in thought light and day light,
lifted up in the mind.
The dark returns to light

36

in the kingfisher's blue and white
richly laid together.
He falls into flight
from the broken ground,
with strident outcry gathers
air under his wings.
In work of love, the body
forgets its weight. And once
again with love and singing
in my mind, I come to what
must come to me, carried
as a dancer by a song.
This grace is gravity.

All *is* Grace

by Henri J. M. Nouwen

RECENTLY TWO FRIENDS of mine left the Daybreak community in Toronto to assume the leadership of another L'Arche community in Canada. The fourteen years that this couple had lived and worked in our community were marked by moments of great joy as well as moments of great sorrow. They had accomplished many beautiful things but also had experienced failure and disappointment; many new friendships had developed, but relationships had been broken as well. During the months before their departure, my friends, together with other members of the community, would say

GREG KING

things like "We are really grateful for all the good things that have happened, for all the beautiful friendships that have developed, for all the hopes that were realized. We simply have to accept or try to forget the painful moments." Listening to comments like these, I began to wonder just exactly what it would mean for my friends to be grateful for their years at Daybreak, and how their gratitude could become the energizing source of their mission.

THE CALL TO GRATITUDE

W E ARE REALLY GRATEFUL for all the good things.... We simply have to accept or try to forget the painful moments." The attitude expressed in these words made me aware of how often we tend to divide our past into good things to remember with gratitude and painful things to accept or forget. Once we accept this division, however, we quickly develop a mentality in which we hope to collect more good memories than bad memories, more things to be grateful for than things to be resentful about, more things to celebrate than things to complain about. But this way of thinking, which at first glance seems quite natural, prevents us from truly allowing our whole past to be the source from which we live our future. Is this the gratitude to which the gospel calls us?

Gratitude in its deepest sense means to live life as a gift to be received gratefully. But gratitude as the gospel speaks about it embraces *all* of life: the good and the bad, the joyful and the painful, the holy and the not so holy. Is this possible in a society where gladness and sadness, joy and sorrow, peace and conflict, remain radically separated? Can we counter the many advertisements that tell us, "You cannot be glad when you are sad, so be happy: buy this, do that, go here, go there and you will have a moment of happiness during which you can forget your sorrow"? Is it truly possible to embrace with gratitude all of our life and not just the good things that we like to remember?

Jesus calls us to recognize that gladness and sadness are never separate, that joy and sorrow really belong together, and that mourning and dancing are part of the same movement. That is why Jesus calls us to be grateful for every moment that we have lived and to claim our unique journey as God's way to mold our hearts to greater conformity with God's own. The cross is the main symbol of our faith, and it invites us to find hope where we see pain and to reaffirm the resurrection where we see death. The call to be grateful is a call to trust that every moment of our life can be claimed as the way of the cross that leads us to new life. When the disciples were on the way to Emmaus and met Jesus, they could not believe that there was much fruit to be expected from all the suffering they had witnessed. But Jesus revealed that it was precisely because of the suffering and pain that new life was born. It is so easy for me to put the bad memories under the rug of my life and to think only about the good things that please me. By doing so, however, I prevent myself from discovering the joy beneath my sorrow, the peace hidden in the midst of my conflicts, and the strength that becomes visible in the midst of my weakness.

THE DISCIPLINE OF GRATITUDE

GRATITUDE is not a simple emotion or an obvious attitude. It is a difficult discipline to constantly reclaim my whole past as the concrete way in which God has led me to this moment and is sending me into the future. It is hard precisely because it challenges me to face the painful moments—experiences of rejection and abandonment, feelings of loss and failure—and gradually to discover in them the pruning hands of God purifying my heart for deeper love, stronger hope, and broader faith. Jesus says to his disciples that although they are as intimately related to him as branches are to the vine, they still need to be pruned in order to bear more fruit (John 15:1-5). Pruning means cutting, reshaping, removing what diminishes vitality. When we look at a pruned vineyard, we can hardly believe it will bear fruit. But when harvest time comes we realize that the pruning enabled the vine to concentrate its energy and produce more grapes than it could have had it remained unpruned. Grateful people are those who can celebrate even the pains of life because they trust that when harvest time comes the fruit will show that the pruning was not punishment but purification.

Gratitude embraces all of life

I am gradually learning that the call to gratitude asks us to say "everything is grace." When our gratitude for the past is only partial, our hope for a new future can never be full. As long as we remain resentful about things that we wish had not happened, about relationships that we wish had turned out differently, about mistakes we wish we had not made, part of our heart remains isolated, unable to bear fruit in the new life ahead of us. To reclaim our history in its totality means that we no longer relate to our past as years in which only good times can be remembered and bad times need to be forgotten, but as opportunities for an ongoing conversion of heart. In a converted heart all of our past can be gathered up in gratitude. If we are to be truly ready for a new task in the service of God, truly joyful at the prospect of a new vocation, truly free to be sent into a new mission, our entire past, gathered into the spaciousness of a converted heart, must become the source of energy that moves us toward the future. It was therefore important that the actual departure of my friends be recognized as the moment in which they could gather up everything they had lived and say, "Thanks be to God." To recollect their history with us as also God's journey with them would set them firmly on the path to their new calling.

THE CELEBRATION OF GRATITUDE

WE MARKED our friends' departure from Daybreak by celebrating the Eucharist. The Eucharist is a celebration in gratitude to God for the divine life among us as a life of suffering as well as joy. As community members sat around the common table and broke bread together to send off our friends with our love, I realized that true gratitude is a profound acknowledgment that every part of our lives, no matter how apparently insignificant or difficult, can be remembered as a part of God's work among us and within us, the work of preparing us yet again for a new mission. The Eucharist, which represents the departure meal of Jesus, is that sacred event that invites us to convert all that has happened in the past into one great wellspring of gratitude and then to move with growing freedom into our future. When Jesus spoke to his disciples before his death and offered them his body and blood as gifts of life, he shared with them everything he had lived—his joy as well as his pain, his suffering as well as his glory—and empowered them to live their mission in deep gratitude.

As we grow older there will be other moments of departure, other opportunities for the Eucharist to teach us gratitude and send us out to new missions. There will always be more to remember and more to gather up in gratitude. And there will always be a new mission: "Love one another as I have loved you" (John 15:12, NRSV).

GRATEFULNESS, THE HEART OF PRAYER. *By Brother David Steindl-Rast. Paulist Press, 997 Macarthur Blvd., Mahwah, NJ 07430, 1984. Pp. 144. Paperback, $8.95. ISBN 0-8091-2628-1.*

THIS BOOK is for all those who would like to enter into abundant life but are uncertain how to do so. With great zest, Brother David points out an often overlooked key to the door—gratitude. In this playful, witty, and gentle book, we are shown how to find and nourish this simple posture of the heart.

Gratitude is something many of us mistake for an arduous work of virtue requiring a felicitous disregard for the actual conditions of our lives. Rather than tackle this calculating, ultimately self-serving misperception head-on, the author sidesteps it by redefining the source of gratitude: It begins, he says, in the experience of surprise. Surprises come in all shapes and sizes, from spectacular celestial events like solar eclipses to the everyday vagaries of the weather. Little or big, welcome or not, every experience of surprise gives us a taste of aliveness, a moment when we feel we have received some message from Life itself.

Once we are conscious of this state of wakefulness, we can work to stay awake and to hear "the great truth that moments of surprise want to teach us: everything is gratuitous, everything is gift." Gratitude is born when our heart says yes to the lesson that God has granted all these occasions of life and is speaking to us through them. It is the song of joy our heart sings for this great gift of life with and in our Maker, and it grows louder and more passionate with every additional moment we are able to stay fully awake to life.

Since these moments of wakefulness are moments of deep contact with God, gratitude is the essence of prayerfulness. And since wakefulness is born of the universal experience of surprise, all prayers are, at a deep level, contemplative in nature. The author thus shows us that the contemplative life is possible (and necessary) for everyone, not just the cloistered. He goes on to illuminate aspects of prayer, discussing the roles of both simple wonderment and concentration in our prayer, the importance and necessity of spiritual leisure, and the relationship between prayer and prayers.

The first half of this book is dedicated to presenting these basic ideas on gratitude, prayer, and contemplation. The second half shows us how to enter the heart of gratefulness through the paths of faith, hope, and love. The author describes how each path leads, by its own route and in cooperation with prayer, to gratitude. He is careful to address common misunderstandings that impede our progress along each path: for faith, fear; for hope, despair; for love, romantic delusions. He concludes with an annotated dictionary of central concepts that recapitulates the central ideas in the book and in places goes beyond them.

This is not always an easy book to read. It is sometimes difficult to follow the connections between the many metaphors and plays on words the author uses to describe concepts, and the language sometimes seems circular and self-contradictory. The difficulty arises from trying to delineate separate features of something that actually is a vast gestalt. At this level of spiritual truth, language is simply inadequate to convey the author's understanding of contemplative realities. Attempts to describe these spiritual realities necessarily appear to the rational mind to involve paradox, something the author acknowledges: "The closer we come to saying something worthwhile, the more likely that paradox will be the only way to express it."

This book can only be fully appreciated by entering its spirit of celebrative playfulness. I found it hard going as long as I tried to wrestle it into a rational exposition. I was only able to understand it by yielding to it. Thus the very style of the book serves its content and can lead us to experience the process through which we begin to live in gratitude.

Rebecca Marnhout

❧

SPACE FOR GOD: STUDY AND PRACTICE OF
SPIRITUALITY AND PRAYER. *By Donald H. Postema.
CRC Publications, 2850 Kalamazoo Ave. SE, Grand Rapids, MI
49560, 1983. Pp. 180. Paperback, $12.95. ISBN 0-933140-46-0.*

IN HER 1986 BOOK *The Protestant Mystics,* Anne Fremantle
reported discovering, in talks with Protestants, that many felt
there were no Protestant mystics at all, except for the Quakers.
Don Postema's *Space for God* helps to correct this misapprehen-
sion. This remarkable book grew out of Postema's year-long
search for the roots of the Reformed understanding of spirituality. He collects in this book the fruits of his far-flung, omnivorous
search among scripture, the writings of John Calvin, Thomas
Merton, and Henri Nouwen, and others; the sayings of the desert
fathers and Hasidic masters; and Dutch and Japanese art. *Space for
God* embraces a whole range of spiritual expression (if we understand spirituality to mean development of a direct relationship to
God) but grounds it all in scripture and the Calvinist tradition of
the theology of sanctification. One might expect some jarring
discords to result from such an enterprise, but Postema masterful-
ly unites all to produce a book that feels consistent, integrated,
and graceful.

Each chapter of *Space for God* begins with a quotation from
the Heidelberg Catechism and other quotations from scripture
and spiritual leaders, combined with a well-chosen painting by
Rembrandt or Van Gogh. There follow three separately titled
sections: *Reflection,* in which Postema writes about the chapter
theme; *Windows of Insight,* in which a collage of short readings,
poems, scripture, and art reproductions illuminates the theme;
and *Exercises,* in which suggestions are given for both group and
individual practice. A wide range of topics is covered, with the
major emphasis resting on gratitude, a theme that runs as a unit-
ing thread through all the chapters. Although the book is suitable
for individual use, its nine chapters could correspond beautifully
to nine group meetings, with encouragement of individual practice and journaling on the days in between meetings.

The author comments, "This book is for busy people who
also want to be deep people," and the suggested exercises bear
this in mind. We are asked to set aside ten or fifteen minutes a
day for reading the Reflection and Windows of Insight sections
within a chapter and five minutes for morning prayer. Later in
the book, evening prayer is also suggested. The author leads us

step by step to get the most out of this time, making suggestions as we go along and encouraging us to develop our own prayer practice, including suggestions for how to do this even in the midst of a busy day.

Space for God is not a book just to read through; rather, it invites participation in prayer at every point. The very format of the book encourages a meditative pace of reading: The layout is spacious and mixes readings, paintings, and poetry among the pages. Each chapter begins with an empty gray page containing a graceful calligraphy chapter number. The use of artwork without accompanying explanatory text leads the reader to read the book intuitively as well as analytically, directly inviting participation of the heart as well as the mind. Postema makes an important contribution by welcoming artists as partners in the spiritual quest.

This book could serve as a helpful introduction to the spiritual life for people in the Reformed tradition who might be searching for spiritual roots but are suspicious of the enterprise. Its grounding in scripture and in Calvinist theology helps make the book feel comfortable to such readers even as it stretches and challenges them. However, it can also provide a refreshing journey for persons of prayer whatever their tradition.

William Moremen

પ્રે

AN INTERRUPTED LIFE—THE DIARIES OF ETTY HILLESUM 1941–43. *Translated by J. G. Gaarlandt. Pocket Books, Simon & Schuster, 1230 Ave. of the Americas, New York, NY 10020, 1988. Pp. 281. Paperback, $4.95. ISBN 0-671-66655-X, WSP.*

ETTY HILLESUM WAS a twenty-seven-year-old Jewish woman living in Amsterdam in 1941 when she began to write the journals and letters that have been excerpted in this volume. The journals cover the period between March 1941 and October 1942 and record Etty's surprising spiritual maturation from a self-involved intellectual into a mystic in deep communion with God. At a time when the Nazi takeover was inspiring terror among Dutch Jews, Etty underwent an amazing inner transformation in the direction of freedom and joy. These journals, collected and kept safe by her admirers, are a remarkable testimony to the sustaining power of faith and prayer.

The earliest entries in the journals reveal little evidence of the enormous growth of spirit Etty was later to sustain. Her life at this point, early in the Nazi occupation, was centered around attempts to come to grips with her identity and her relationships with others. Though her everyday life was still largely stable, her inner life was full of passionate turmoil. Her emotional life came to revolve around one man, Julius Spier, an analyst who had studied with Carl Jung and who, by all accounts, possessed rare psychological insight. Etty became his assistant and later his lover and intellectual partner.

During the time when Etty's life was largely consumed by her life with Spier, friendships among the coterie of admirers surrounding him, and her writing, the Nazi oppression of Dutch Jews progressively worsened. By April 1942 they were forced to wear the Star of David, and wholesale deportation began later that spring. As her external world succumbed to the chaos and uncertainty of war, her inner world evolved in the direction of serenity and security. The agency of this change was her increasingly intense dialogue with God, undergirded by a rather eclectic mixture of Judaism and Christianity that nevertheless was the vehicle for a wholly pure faith.

We watch her summon up powers of spirit we might never have guessed resided within her, as she calmly and boldly faces the Jews' destruction at the hands of the Nazis. While gazing steadily at the hardships that she and others around her suffer, she is able to proclaim a deep faith in the goodness of life: "Something has crystallized. I have looked our destruction, our miserable end which has already begun in so many small ways in our daily life, straight in the eye and accepted it into my life, and my love of life has not been diminished." That love of life leads her to repeat again and again her commitment not to be consumed by hatred and her deep gratitude to God "for leaving me so free of bitterness and hate."

As the days went on, she found herself moving more and more into constant prayer. When the movements of Jews were restricted, she was confined for long periods to her study. However, her soul could not be so confined, and she recorded feeling that even in the smallest space she knew that she would be able to pray. When others around her could think only about having fallen into the clutches of the Nazis, she asserted that she was not in anyone's clutches but was safe in God's arms. Rather than blaming God for allowing the Nazi occupation, she proclaimed that believers must help God by constantly protecting God's dwelling place within.

> *The jasmine behind my house has been completely ruined by the rains and storms of the last few days, its white blossoms are floating about in muddy black pools on the low garage roof. But somewhere inside me the jasmine continues to blossom undisturbed, just as profusely and delicately as ever it did. And it spreads its scent round the House in which You dwell, oh God. You can see, I look after You, I bring You not only my tears and my forebodings on this stormy, grey Sunday morning, I even bring you scented jasmine. . . . I shall try to make You at home always. Even if I should be locked up in a narrow cell and a cloud should drift past my small barred window, then I shall bring you that cloud, oh God, while there is still the strength in me to do so.*

Finally, in August 1942, she was consigned with her family to the internment camp of Westerbork, from which Jews and other "undesirables" were deported to Auschwitz on a weekly basis. Etty stayed in the camp until September 1943. Her spiritual life there became immensely concentrated; she commented that her first two months behind barbed wire had been the richest and most intense months of her life. In the midst of the squalor, the confinement, the fear, she praised God for life, for beauty, for the secure refuge of her soul. By this time she had come to see that the task of life, in good times and bad, was not to "make the best of things" but to know within oneself that everything *is* fine just as it is.

Etty's journals end after her first few months at Westerbork, but several letters included in the book chronicle the events of the rest of her year there. The beauty and freedom of her inner life shined out amid the dark terror and anguish of her fellow prisoners. Seemingly endless love and goodness welled up from the sacred spring in her heart, and she freely shared these living waters with her campmates. Her prayers in these last days of her life consisted of intense expressions of gratitude and passionate offerings to God of every earthly and spiritual beauty that she could gather:

You have made me so rich, oh God, please let me share out Your beauty with open hands. My life has become an uninterrupted dialogue with You, oh God, one great dialogue. Sometimes when I stand in some corner of the camp, my feet planted on Your earth, my eyes raised towards Your Heaven, tears sometimes run down my face, tears of deep emotion and gratitude. At night, too, when I lie in my bed and rest in You, oh God, tears of gratitude run down my face, and that is my prayer.

Etty's spirit glowed brightly to the end. She stepped onto the deportation train "talking gaily, smiling, a kind word for everyone she met on the way, full of sparkling humour, perhaps just a touch of sadness," as the chronicler of her last day in the camp describes. Later, some farmers along the train route discovered a postcard she had thrown out of the train. "We have left the camp singing," it said. Etty Hillesum died in Auschwitz on November 30, 1943.

Judith E. Smith

ﺰ